DUAL CITIZEN

A Ghanaian Canadian Memoir

Kwame Stephens

Dedication
To Araba Sarkwa, Adwoa Sarkwa and Eliska

CONTENTS

Preface

Most persons living in Canada migrated here or are descendants of immigrants. That's unless of course, you are Native Canadian. This land that some of us call home has been yours going back before time began.

This memoir is about my immigrant journey and how thirty years later, I have come to peace with the complexity of accepting my being a dual citizen. My migration started in Accra, Ghana, West Africa. It ended in Toronto, Ontario, Canada. What transpired after that is what makes my story unique and maybe not that special. This book is poetic, prosaic and photographic.
As I let you into intimate moments and periods of my life, I trust that you will find glimpses of yours. I have often found that part of what makes being an immigrant to a new world enjoyable is sharing and telling of our stories.

Me da ase. Thank You.
Kwame Stephens

Migration

Even though it's been over thirty years, that day feels like yesterday. It was in early March in the late 1980s. My migration to Canada from Ghana began with my departure from Kotoka International Airport Accra. Planning for my move to Canada had started a decade before when my older and only brother came to Canada to study. At the time he had said, "I'll bring you over once I settle down." My life continued after that comment. I'd go to university, study, graduate, work etc. All the while knowing that my brother would have me join him in Canada sometime in the future. At the time he made that promise, I was in my late teens doing my A' Levels in Nairobi where my father was working at the time. I'm not sure what twists and turns my brother went through to get to the point of being able to sponsor me, but he did it. He honoured his promise.

At the time of my migration, the world then was not ruled by personal computers. We had typewriters. I had learnt WordPerfect before leaving Ghana but I did not own a personal computer. I used to write in a journal in those days. A page from my journal is shown here.

The night before I was scheduled to leave Ghana, I wrote some thoughts down. I was not coming directly to Canada. The next day, I boarded an Ethiopian Airlines jet that would take me to

Nairobi to visit my father and older sister for three weeks before heading to Toronto.

I wrote the poem below in my journal.

when dawn breaks

tomorrow, when the dawn breaks
I will be miles away
on my way to a new land
quite different from this one

tomorrow, when the dawn breaks
dear friends and loved ones
will be miles away
our times together will become
a memory to be cherished
tomorrow, when the dawn breaks
I will feel all alone like a ship
lost out at sea

tomorrow, when the dawn breaks
my mind will be racing
it will be in a state of panic
or a state of tension
asking questions like
'what does future hold'?
can I brave the storms of life?'
and many more

tomorrow, when the dawn breaks
and I am miles away
and dear friends and loved ones are gone

and I'm all alone
and my mind is racing
thank you, Jesus
that you will be there
so that I can talk to you
share my feelings with you
trust in you

yes, tomorrow when the breaks
Jesus will be there
to guide me and lead
to help me build a new life
to give me the strength to face the challenges
that will surely come my way

My farewell "party" at Kotoka International Airport was a small one. My mother was there with my dearest paternal Auntie. Here's a photo of the three of us before I bid adieu to Ghana.

I was excited about what lay ahead when I left Ghana. Going to Kenya was not a big deal. I had gone back often to Kenya since completing my A'Levels and returning to study at Kwame Nkrumah University of Science and Technology (KNUST), Kumasi in the late 1970's. Kenya is my second home on the African continent. I pride myself in speaking broken Kiswahili. Thanks to my father's work, I went to primary school in Zambia from the late 1960's to early 1970's. I'd gotten to see ten African countries in total. If there are two things that shape the nuclear family I was born into, they are travel and education. I celebrated my eighteenth birthday in England. At that time my father had a ritual that when a child of his turned eighteen, they were given a ticket and then put on a plane to go and visit London. I'd gone through that rite about a decade before my migration to Canada. Canada was going to be the last stop for this roving man. The reluctant child traveller who was now a man was going to put down some roots.

My visit to Kenya was short and sweet. My older sister was there. Daddy had moved from the larger home we lived in at Adam's Arcade on Ngong Road in earlier years to a smaller apartment. It was then that I realized that my father had aged.

Before leaving for Canada, my father gave me a US $20.00 bill. The man who had trained me on budgeting by giving me pocket money from childhood to adulthood wanted to make sure that on my trip to Canada, I had funds to spend on incidentals. My father also handed me a thick winter jacket. Over his many years of travelling around the world, Dad had come to Canada. He knew that I would need that brown suede jacket with a dark brown mane to keep me warm until I bought my own. Daddy was doing what he had done for my life…Educate, feed and clothe…as any responsible parent did.

It was in March 1989 when I made my first Trans Atlantic flight from Amsterdam to Toronto. I remember looking below from the plane and seeing fields of white snow. I'd seen snow before. It snows in Lesotho in Southern Africa where I visited twice in my teens. What freaked me out was the "snow as far as my eyes could go". When I was coming to Canada, the cold was the only thing that I was worried about because that triggers my asthma. Eventually, structures appeared and we landed safely at Pearson International Airport. I was glad to see my older brother and his wife waiting for me in the Arrival Lounge. I'd finally arrived safely in Canada. I was experiencing the start of my life in the "new world". My mindset then was that I had come here with a one-way ticket. No more moving around as I had in my childhood. Canada was going to be my permanent home.

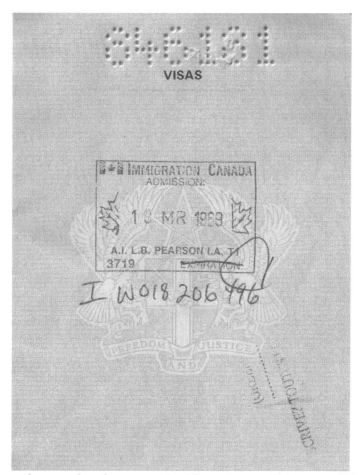

That was then and today my mind has changed about calling Canada home for life. This book is about my journey to becoming a dual Ghanaian Canadian Citizen. Let's go on this journey, this *akwantu*, together. Meet the people I've met, lessons I've learned, feelings I've felt and so much more.

Myths Vs Reality

During the process of having my Landed Immigrant papers processed, I'd visit the Canadian High Commission in Accra regularly. There was a staff member there called Ms. Kerr and I'd keep telling her on my visits that "I really want to have a white Christmas this year." My understanding then was that a white Christmas meant celebrating the Yule Tide in Canada with Caucasian people. I'd heard the Bing Crosby classic but I was misguided. I had no idea that a White Christmas happened when it snowed on Christmas day! This was one of the many misconceptions and myths about Canada I arrived here with. After I got to Canada, I had a reality check about my preconceived ideas. Here are some of those myths that were debunked after my migration.

The Cold For me the formula as simple. Canada = Cold. All the time, all year round. Imagine my disdain during my first summer when it was hotter in Toronto than Accra. I mean it. On a hot day in Accra, the coastal breeze reduces the humidity. You don't only want an air conditioner in July and August in Canada. You need one. Fans don't cut it here. They simply blow around the hot humid air.

Bilingualism In the months leading up to my departure from Ghana – via Kenya to Canada, I enrolled in French courses at Alliance Francaise in Accra. I bought into the great Canadian marketing myth that everyone here spoke both French and English fluently. After all the whole country was bilingual right? Don't get me wrong, I knew some French back in those days. In my secondary school days in Ghana, with the country surrounded by three French-speaking nations, we were all required to study three years of French. Imagine my shock on arrival to realize when I said "Bonjour" the response was often "Bon who?". No regrets for keeping up my French though. On my trips to Montreal or Quebec City, my basic French comes in handy. In Ontario though, it's pretty useless. Unless when I go to a government building or see the signs on the highways.

Christianity in Canada Back in my early years in Canada, I was a committed practicing born again Evangelical Christian. It took three tries to catch the only GO bus from Richmond Hill where I lived then with my brother into Toronto. This bus passed the stop at quarter to each hour. I was not used to such a schedule. In Ghana when you wanted a bus, you normally stood at a spot and waited for one to come. The concept of a rigid schedule was new to me. I finally made it to this big church that my mother bragged about after her previous trips to Canada before I arrived. I did what any good Christian in Ghana would do after the service. I asked for a church elder and explained that I wanted to know if any members lived in Richmond Hill. If someone could give me a ride on Sundays. In Ghana, this would be the normal thing to do. Christians were loving and sharing and caring. If need be, a family in Ghana would overload their car to accommodate my request. Everyone looked at me weirdly when I started asking for what I thought was a small favour, so I stopped asking. I realized that in "self-sufficient" Canada, Christianity was practiced differently than we did in Ghana where we share the little we had. This and other factors would shake my faith and later lead me to be "less born again" with time. Talk about culture shock. This was spiritual shock that shook my faith to the core.

Race Matters Way before arriving in Canada, there were some white American Baptist missionaries in Cape Coast Ghana – where I stayed. Even in my twenties at that time I knew about racism in North America. I'd bring this up with these missionaries. They kept saying, "Racism is like a blind spot". As though it was a spec in the culture here. It didn't take long after coming to the western world for me to realize how much of a myth that was. I had my first direct experience of racism while in transit at Schipol Airport in Amsterdam. I was waiting in line to be served. The server ignored me until a white man insisted that he attend to me. In a more recent situation during training with a group of strangers, a comment was made to insinuate that I was a thief. Racism seems to be so deeply woven in the fabric of western society. Most "visible minorities" - who are apparently becoming the majority - deal with it in different ways. I pick and choose when to react to what I see as overt racism. Sometimes I ignore what happens. Sometimes I use what happens to educate. Sometimes I go full-on "Let me tell you something!"

Race ties into an idea I had before arriving about Canada not having that many black people here. All the images I saw of Canada before arriving was that of white people. On my way here, by virtue of my brother being here, I was sure that there were other Ghanaians and Africans in Canada. What I never realized was how large the Caribbean population in Canada is. Not to mention Black Canadians who have been here for generations upon generations. How come no one ever tells you that about all these people when you see the videos of the Mounties and the blink of First Nations Canadians? There is a plethora of blackness from so many backgrounds and shades in Canada that I continue to be exposed to.

The first three years in Canada were the most difficult for me. There were many adjustments. Much as I'd travelled a lot before arriving here, it took a while to get used to how precisely time was kept here. The idea of looking a person in the eye and not nodding or acknowledging them when you saw them in the street was odd to me too. This was the normal thing to do back then in Ghana. I was fortunate to have come to this country as a skilled Architectural Designer and able to land a job in a month. I got my car within a year. Staying with my older brother for my first three years helped ease things. The bond I shared with him and especially my oldest niece was special and remains to this day. My brother shared a lot of wisdom he'd gained from starting in Canada as a struggling student and eventually becoming a working professional. Some of the best advice he gave was "let your fingers do the walking", "There's no free lunch in North America", "Buy a property. Don't pay rent forever". I took those words to heart and they went a long way. I eventually moved out of my brother's home and lived on my own. Not long after that, I became a Canadian citizen.

The day after taking the Oath of Citizenship I went to my day job to find a cake my coworkers had gotten with lots of Canadian flags on it. I was Canadian finally three years in. My younger nephew was born around the time I left my brother's home. At that time I wrote a poem with him in mind, wondering what lay ahead for him as a black boy born here in Canada. Here is the poem inspired by my now very successful nephew.

Prayer for the Black Child

this is for the black child
born in this country
born into this world
that may help him grow up

this is for the black child
who before the age of twelve
may have a criminal record
for a crime he did not commit

this is for the black child
who will have to struggle
against a white wall
all through his days on earth

this is for the black child
who may grow up into

an angry black man
who hates a world which hates him
>if there is something
>you or I can do
>for this black child
>then let us do it
>whatever it is
>may we do our part
>to make this world
>a better place
>a safer place
>for the black child

The First Ten Years

*S*it back now and enjoy the newsreel version of the first ten years. FADE IN

I have arrived in Canada at last. I'm eager to work. My brother gives me lots of advice about living in Canada. He's urging me to take it easy after my long trip. I'm not in that mode. I start going out of the house in Richmond Hill which back in the late '80s lacks the kind of transit Toronto had. I find the library which is half an hour walk away from where we live. I find out the fastest way for me to find a job is through an Employment Agency. With my brother's help, we find one in my field. Architecture. The man there likes me. He changes my CV (Curriculum Vitae) into a North American resume. He likes the drafting skills I have. Construction and the economy in Canada are booming. The agency man sends me as the first person for an interview at Shoppers Drug Mart Head Office in the DVP and Sheppard area. I ace the interview and land the job within a month of my arrival. Not bad I think to myself. My starting pay is $10.50/hour. I remember my new boss telling me to always look busy. "That's how they'll keep you hired". A lesson that has stayed with me all these years. The drafting job I'm doing is to fill in during the summer. I write the slogan "Savings, service, selection – everything you want in a drug a store" over and over again." I'm shocked when I get my first paycheck. What's this big chunk they take off called taxes? I didn't know that this thing called taxes are taken off my pay will get worse and worse. Now that I have money, I start exploring. Go up the CN Tower several times. Visit the Ontario Science Centre, Niagara Falls. I buy a book about Toronto's many parks and trails. I buy a racing bike with my first credit card from Canadian Tire. I am living the Canadian dream. I have started to build a credit history without knowing it. I stay in touch with my parents in Ghana by phone. As I continue to work, I am exposed to another kind of culture shock. The fact that you can work with someone for the whole day but when they see you outside, they don't know you.This is so un-Ghanaian to me. Welcome to Canada. I adapt. My brother who knows that I know how to drive insists that I get a driver's license. I'm hesitant. I don't want to.The introverted me in those days. With encouragement, I go and buy the book. You know? The one where you study to take the written test? I take the written test eventually and fail. I lick my wounds. I study harder and pass it the second time. The insurance guy I am introduced to tells me that I have to take Driver Education Classes to get 3 or so years driving credit. I do. I take the road test and pass – even though the examiner tells me that I need more practice with my parallel parking. The driver's license opens new doors. The purchase of a car. Driving to see friends in DC. Flying to California to see an old school mate. Renting cars. Eventually, the summer job ends. I have taken a course called "AutoCAD for Architects" at Ryerson Polytechnic as the guy at the Employment Agency suggested. I see an ad for a job with Mr. Submarine…I am about to go for the interview wearing the jacket my father gave me - with my suit coat sticking about three inches below the hem of the winter jacket. My only friend outside work – a Ghanaian graduate student who my brother had introduced me to – gives me his London Fog coat which covers everything. Now I'm looking Canadian, not a recently arrived immigrant who doesn't know how to dress. I pass the job interview and get my first "permanent job". The job is amazing while it lasts.

We often get free baseball game tickets. Right behind the pitcher at the SkyDome. I learn Canadian geography because I do drawings for Mr. Sub stores all around Canada. I try skating with one of

my coworkers at Mr. Sub. I make a good friend that I'm still close to until this day. The "permanent job" lasts about nineteen months until the economy tanks and I get laid off from Mr. Submarine. During that time though, England is a short flight away so I fly there often. I eventually move to Toronto…First I live in a shared house. Then on my own. Takes a few tries to find an apartment I like at Bathurst and St. Clair. One day I see an ad looking for night school instructors. They want someone to teach interior decorating. I go for the Information Session and tell them I can do that. Well, I now have to study to teach this. Over the years, I teach Interior Decorating with Toronto District School Board, Catholic School Board and York Region school board. I'm the greedy immigrant who has come to this country to work hard. Sometime after being laid off from my "permanent job" I see an ad looking for Volunteer Probation officers. I am curious. I go for another Information session, interview and soon I am monitoring cases for persons on Probation. I learn more about the underbelly of Canadian society. This volunteer position eventually leads to my current job with a Community Organization…I got the job by responding to an ad in the Toronto Star. Just before being told I had been hired, out of desperation and my Employment Insurance running out, I drive my car from Etobicoke in the west of Toronto to Scarborough in the east. I apply to a lot of Security Jobs. I work as a security guard for just a month before I quit to start my real job. In that first decade here, my parents visit and as they don't stay with me, I visit them regularly where they are staying. I even take my mother to church sometimes. Talking of which, coming to Canada means that for the first time in my adult life I am exposed to people from other faiths. The first religious book I read outside Christianity is about the Bahai faith. I start seeing the world differently. I start exploring…All kinds of things. Thanks to a Vietnamese friend I get into Asian food. Then Jamaican food. Toronto, the multicultural city allows me to go way beyond myself not only food-wise but creatively, culturally, emotionally, sexually and in so many ways. I dabble here and there and continue to explore. Meanwhile, my mother is bent on getting me married. She has me meet the daughter of a good friend of hers who is visiting Toronto. Nothing comes out of that. The first time I read poetry to the public is at a Talent show. I read three poems and I am then on hooked on doing this. Performing and reading poetry leads to writing theatrical sketches, stage-plays and more. That is how the first ten years I spent in Canada whizzes by... in a nutshell.

FADE TO BLACK

Footnotes

One day
when I write the story of my life
there will be many chapters
and many many more footnotes

The chapters
will be the big chunks of my life
childhood, adolescence, adulthood
and so on

But what will be
the most important
will be the Footnotes

Each Footnote
will be someone
who touched my life
in one way or another

Some Footnotes
will the friends long gone
the ones you think about

and say "I wonder what
happened to so and so"

Some Footnotes
will be good friends you once had
but somehow you drifted apart

Some Footnotes
will be lovers you once had
where the love turned to hate

One day
when I write the story of my life
there will be many many important
Footnotes

Places I Remember

Now that you've read the newsreel, here are some photos that go with the words.

I did the drive down to the Washington D.C. Area to visit a school mate from KNUST several times. God bless my 1990 Dodge Shadow that took me and brought me back so often.

"Officer am I under arrest?" This photo was taken on one of my visits to England were to see my younger sister there.

My first California vacation in 1996 was by far one of my best vacations ever. That was thanks to a classmate of mine from Kenya who planned it.

Imagine sleeping in a car then waking up, driving and creeping up on the Golden Gate Bridge. Amazing!

On the way to get some seafood at the Outer Banks.

Vancouver, British Columbia

Lunenburg   On a wine tour
Nova Scotia   in California

Return To Ghana

Great Tree

A great tree has fallen
in the forest, just outside Elmina*

A great tree has fallen
one that was rooted in Africa
but whose branches spanned
across the world to every continent
and touched the lives of all mankind

A great tree has fallen
a great tree whose leaves provided shade
for many, whose trunk gave strength to numerous
whose roots grounded millions, who's height inspired us all
yes, this tree has graced the earth that it lived on
for over seventy years

A great tree has fallen
and we are gathered here
to honour him and take heed
and learn from the blessing of his life

Elmina is my hometown

Closing Time

Closing time, five o'clock
Friday, first October 1999
He breathed his last gasp of air

the consummate bureaucrat
the strong patriarch of the clan
has laid down his mantle
at five o'clock
on Friday

he lived a bureaucrat
and died a mover and shaker
organizing, delegating duties
as he made his grand exit
on his terms, his way

now he's moved on
to another world
to once again start working
on new tasks given him

It's five o'clock now
thank God it's the weekend
time to rest from his labour

My father passed away on Friday, October 1st, 1999 at 5.00 p.m. That's when I was inspired to write the two poems above. In my eyes, Daddy was a great man. Even though he lived on earth for just over seventy years he did way more than most who have lived longer. He was many things to many people. To me, he was "Dadda". Not necessarily a friend but a father and a provider. I had spoken to him two weeks before he passed away. In that conversation, he urged me to go back to school. Yes, I had a Bachelor's Degree in Architectural Design from Kwame Nkrumah University of Science and Technology. Yes, I had a good job but in his mind, because I had not done the requisite Post Graduate Diploma to become an architect, he felt his job as a parent wasn't complete. Just so you know Dadda, I recently obtained a Master Certificate in Adult Development and Training from Schulich School Business/ York University. I hope wherever you are that satisfies your educational desires for me – your second son.

I went back to Ghana for my father's funeral about a month later. That was over ten years after my migration to Canada on what I was sure was a one-way ticket. It had been ten years of settling in. Finding jobs in the architectural field for three years. Then with the recession at the time being laid off. I eventually landed a more secure job in a totally different field. Thanks, Dadda that the amazing education you ensured that I and your four other children received allowed me to be flexible and ready for change. Ten years in Canada had led me to change. My life had opened up to the many things Canada had to offer. New experiences that I didn't know existed. Unlike some who may come to this country and stay amongst "their own", I took the Ontario vehicle number plate moto "Yours to discover" seriously. I went beyond the walls of being born again to being more broad in how I saw life. I came to terms with my authentic self, not the one imposed on me by a program of tradition. I was 90% Canadian and the rest was "whatever".

So much went on during the two and half week trip to Ghana. I missed Canada my new home and wanted to come back to the apartment I stayed in at Bathurst and St. Claire West in Toronto so badly. I found the trip and family events around my father's funeral tiring and tedious. These were things I had been shielded from as a child. My parents raised us in cities, not in villages fraught with all kinds of social norms. There seemed to be rituals for everything. How you greeted people seated in a circle. Which hand you used. Idioms that made references to the Fanti language (my mother tongue) and culture that I had no clue meant. Ghana at that time was not much different from how I'd left it a decade before. The economy appeared to be in shambles. I must say my views of Ghana softened up at the many social gatherings we attended. I met friends I'd not seen for ages. I visited my grandmother who I had grown up with. I got back in touch with my roots – the boarding school I'd gone to. I reconnected with my mother, sisters, cousins, aunts, uncles and so many others. Maybe the ten years in Canada had also caused me to mature. I was about to hit the big forty a few years later. Life was more grey than black and white as I'd seen it in my earlier life.

We held my father's funeral service at Christ The King Cathedral in Accra on a Friday morning. My dearest Auntie Mary played the organ for her brother's goodbye. The church was packed and I saw lots of classmates and friends I'd not seen for a while. My mother reverted to her youth when she saw an old classmate from her days at Holy Child High School. Who knows what mischief those two got up to in those younger days? You could see the glint in their eyes when they greeted, embraced and called each other by nicknames only they understood the meanings of. My father's body was taken to Elmina where he was laid to rest. The day after, the family attended a service at St. Joseph's Church in Elmina. At the service, I heard a priest preach for twenty minutes in the purest Fanti I'd ever heard. The only English word he used in the entire twenty minutes was "platform". Most people like myself mix a lot of English into our Fanti. This priest's command of the language was spectacular.

It was at the Thanksgiving Service in Accra a week later that my Auntie Mary introduced me to the daughter of a good friend. I was at an age where "the program" said I should be married. Matchmaking continued.

This trip to Ghana led me to the house in Ghana where my father spent his years of retirement. I had heard about the house but had never been in it. The first time I went to the house was to see my father's dead body lying there in the living room as we shared stories about what he meant to us outside.

Returning to Toronto after this trip was a relief. I was still on the path of staying true to my goal of becoming Canadian and never wanting to go back to Ghana for good. No change there. I was at the stage in my life though where I was creating strong bonds with people that I often refer to as "chosen family". People I'd met through work, volunteering or the arts who had become like family to me. Sometimes they have been closer and dearer than blood family.

Here are two poems about my father. I sent him the first one while he was living. The second poem is a reflection piece I wrote after he had left us.

a son, a man, a boy

He lost a son but gained a man
he lost the boy he could boss around
lay guilt trips on and a good "yes dad" boy
he lost one, he could treat as a pawn
in this weird schema called family

yet, he gained a man
a man who can stand tall
with his head held high before crowds
a man who could strike his breast and say
"yes, me, my way," without regret or remorse
a man who loves a world that loves him too

yet, can this dad accept this man?
can he look this man eyeball to eyeball
and show him the love, respect
and dignity he deserves

he lost a son, yet the world gained a man
a nobleman, a brave man, a caring man
and maybe he may never know the friendship

of this man, for in his eyes
the boy will always be just a boy

Conversations We Never Had

If I could see you now
I'd talk to you man to man
Not son to father as we have in the past

If I could see you now
I'd say thank you...thank you
for being the best father you knew how to be.

First, you stepped up to the plate
I knew you from the day I was born
Not only did I know you, you clothed me
fed me, made sure I went to school, university
and then some

I'd thank you for
doing all you could to make my early years easier for me
at times when we were miles away from the land of my birth
for whatever your reasons were, even though I do not know
you chose to part ways with Mum

I'd thank you Dad for moments that always stand out
When I got burnt, you were there
When I was unwell, you were there
When I needed to drive, you taught me to reverse
There are many moments that I remember

If you were here right now
I'd ask you some difficult questions
Things I don't understand about you.

Why Daddy? Why Daddy? Why Daddy?
would you seek to tear down people dear to me?
Why all the liaisons you had with this one and that one
Why did you not treat each of your children the same?

31

October 1972. Robert had taken his life in desperation at Epsom College... the sixteen lad wrote, "I know if daddy were here everything would be all right for me!" He wanted to move to a Day School. Daddy, alas, if you were here? three thousand miles away. did not understand the anguish of the stress through which the lad was passing.

Why did you always want more and more
when we couldn't give it?
There are more questions that I have but these will do for now

Daddy, my Daddy, If you were here now
I'd tell you that I kinda understand you
As I get up every morning, I remember how
you would get up every morning at eight on the dot
You worked and worked just to keep us living well
You must have been lonely at times
as you took care of others' problems
Daddy, I want to let you know
I understand you now

Daddy, my Daddy, As I journey on
and look in the mirror and see the image of me
which is the exact image of you
I understand that family is important
and you knew how to hold us together
all five kids, even when we warred

Daddy, my Daddy, As I age
I understand that you had concerns
coz we all do, you drew on the God you knew
and I draw on mine too to see me through
life's many changes

Daddy, my Daddy, if you were here now
I'd have us sit in my solarium and get you some beer
coz I know you loved yours
We'd look back at those moments we shared
how you strived to lay a solid foundation in me
of family, living within my means, the value of friends and more
I'd show you what I've been able to do with my life
and where I'm heading, I'd ask for your advice
coz sometimes I wish you were here

Yeah Daddy, if you were here,

We start to have a conversation
The first of many conversations we never had

For The Love Of Mother & Ghana

After going to Ghana to lay my father to rest, I came back to Canada to pursue my Canadian dreams. I was doing well. I bought a luxury condominium.

I'd gone to see my mother in England from Canada where she was spending time with my younger sister in that period. The poem below was written in tears on the flight back to Canada. My mother's mortality hit me then for the first time. Mamma, my rock, my soul my heart was growing old.

Walking Together

I remember her
in the prime of her life
I used to walk with her
down the road with her
proud of her... loving her
thinking to myself, "that's my first lady
my special woman and my sweet mother"

> and as I walked down the road with her recently
> on the streets of London, her grey hair
> creeping out from under her brown wig
> I knew she was still my special woman
> and I love her so and am really proud of her

her hands were feeble
she couldn't see too well
without her glasses
that she'd forgotten
to bring along

> I walked with her, beside her
> talking and thinking
> "you will always be my first lady
> and I will always love you"

then she said in her firm voice
"It was nice to walk with you"
and I thought to myself
"mummy you are still my first lady,
my special woman and my sweet mother"
and in my heart, we will always be
walking together

Everything was business as usual after that. I was in touch on the phone with my mother frequently after the visit. She always seemed calm and her voice seemed strong. Things changed when one day my brother came back from a trip to Ghana and showed me photos of my mother. The images are still ingrained in my mind today. My beloved mother looked gaunt and lean. The photos came with a dire warning.

"Mamma is not looking good and who knows what may happen to her? You may want to go and see her in Ghana soon." I did what any good son would do. I requested time from work and in February 2006, I was on two Lufthansa jets heading to Ghana to see my beloved mother.

I have always been very close to my mother. As a child, I had severe asthma and other medical problems. My mother would take me from doctor to doctor when I got sick. My mother was always there for me. Even though I was the third of my parent's four children, I was treated as the last born. I was my Mum's declared favourite. My mother used to call me "me ba" – My child.

My brother made sure that my visit to Ghana was paved with rose petals. On arrival at Kotoka International Airport Accra, I was met by one of my older brother's good friends. I had my own driver and personal aid along with a Toyota Corolla at my disposal. Driving from the airport, I immediately noticed that things had changed in Ghana since my trip in 1999. The main roads were better paved. When I was growing up in the '60s and '70s we'd travel to other African countries, people would ask "what side of the road do you drive on in Ghana". I'd jokingly respond that we drove on the left, right or middle depending on where the potholes were. It looked as though we were actually driving on the right side this time. There were positive changes in Ghana and I was glad to see that.

From the late 1960s until my departure from Ghana to Canada in 1989, Ghana had been through quite a few military and civilian regimes. Life was difficult for most people and basic products – then called "essential commodities" - were hard to find. Most stores were bare. The most popular brand of soap was Lux if you were wealthy. You bathed using cheap Key Soap if you were not well off. Toothpaste of choice? Pepsodent. Milk brand? The most popular was Ideal/Carnation milk. These were some of the essential commodities. I remember my father sharing a story of seeing a line during those hard times in Ghana's history. You would first join the line as he did, then asking what the line up for. The line up my father joined that day was for dolls. I've always wondered if my father left the line or stayed to buy a doll.

We made our way home from the airport through the widened paved roads. I woke up early the next morning waiting for the driver. He was supposed to come and take me on the four or so hour drive to Takoradi to see my mother. I was still on North American time thinking he'd be punctual. I gradually relaxed and asked the house help to get me a Star Lager – even though it was before noon. This was my wind-down. My disengaging from my Canadian self and remembering that I was now in Ghana. A different place. The values we have in Canada are not the same as some people have in Ghana. This also made me realize that I was now truly living the "dual life". Despite this difference internally, outwardly I blended in amongst other reasons because I looked like everyone and spoke Fanti. I was falling in love with this new Ghana. I was enjoying this change of pace.

The driver arrived eventually. He proved to be skillful as he maneuvered us through the widened four-lane highway as we left Accra and drove to Takoradi. On arrival there, I was glad to see my mother who was very much alive and well. I was glad to talk to her. Hold her hand. Catch up with her. Pray with her. Eat with her. No amount of phone calls can make up for seeing your own mother in the flesh. (This was before the time video chatting was popular). I spent two weeks with my mother and it was nice to have some alone time. Mum was always good on advise. She asked about work. She encouraged me to learn about computers even though she was not savvy with them. Mum loved watching CNN and discussing world affairs. She had a knack of getting me to laugh with her comments and one-liners. Steeped in her Bible

Mum reminded me to read mine. She showed me some of her favourite Psalms. She knew some of these by heart and while we were home, she'd be saying them as she walked around. It was good to be around this strong spiritual woman.

I realized at the time that my mother – much as she had birthed four of us – may have primarily been a loner. My parents had separated in the '60s and my father had left the country with me and some siblings. That's when Mum moved to Takoradi where she was close to her family. My mother was retired now. When it was time to leave and after the long goodbye, my driver who had been waiting for me took us to Harbourview. Harbourview is a restaurant-bar that overlooks Takoradi Harbour. He then took me to Ghana Secondary Technical School – aka GSTS.

GSTS. Where I was in boarding school from twelve to seventeen years old. Upon returning to Ghana after six years of primary education in Zambia this was where my parents decided this would be a good school for me to attend. They could tell I was creative already then. Not only that, my mother was nearby so if anything happened to me healthwise, she would be there. One of my Uncles – the closest/younger brother of my mother - was nearby in Sekondi. The five years in GSTS deserve a whole book. They were filled with turmoil around religion, sexuality and adapting to Ghana after being in Zambia. In that period my siblings and I visited Lesotho where Dad was based. He had moved there after living in Zambia. For two summers, we were put on a Pan Am jet at Kotoka International airport where we flew directly to Johannesburg's Jan Smuts Airport. We would fly from there locally to Bloemfontein where my father would drive from Maseru Lesotho to meet us and take us home. My experiences in South Africa in the 1970s were my taste of apartheid. That bitter taste still remains. When we got into the airport at Johannesburg and we were on the international side, we were human. When we crossed into the domestic side for our second flight, the "White" and "Non-White" signs appeared. Or as I remember them so many years later, "Blankie" and "Ni Blankie" (Please forgive my broken Afrikaans).

We left Takoradi and spent a few nights in Elmina the hometown. The country air was cleaner than in Accra. It was nice to wake up to cocks crowing. After the stopover, we went on to Accra. As I unwound from the road trip, my dedicated driver suggested that we take an excursion to Aburi where he was from. I had heard about Aburi Gardens while growing up but never been there. Being a tourist in Zambia, Kenya, Lesotho and other African countries I'd been to was normal. In Ghana, I had done limited tourist stuff. At Aburi I got to drink fresh palm wine as this photo shows.

I left Ghana this time around with a desire to come back soon because I felt a new connection. The roots I'd left behind seemed closer. I was discovering Ghana through the eyes of a visiting Canadian – wanting to explore more. Ghana had changed. The country appeared to have become more like North America. To cap it all, the place was more politically stable. My one-way ticket plans to Canada had started to be derailed.

My desire to return more often was reinforced the day I returned to Toronto after over twenty hours of travel. The taxi ride from the airport was quiet as the driver's focus was on the highways. I surmised that if this was in Ghana, I would be striking a conversation with the taxi driver in my mother tongue or a similar language. I made it home tired and got my condo keys from the gatehouse. After swiping the access card to open the door to the building, a Caucasian woman rushed ahead of me and scooted up one of the elevators without waiting for me. I felt like I had just been treated like "another black man". This stung me. I got up to my condo apartment and immediately called my brother in the United States. I told him, "I just got back to Canada and I want to go back to Ghana." His response was, "You may want to think of finding ways to make your return more permanent or frequent." His words resonated deeply with me.

In Memoriam

Soon after settling down into my routine in Toronto, I was informed that my brother's father-in-law was extremely sick and in hospital. Paapa, as we affectionately called him, was a close family friend. Both our families had lived in Zambia. Paapa and my father were well-travelled Ghanaian expatriates. Paapa was a father to me. I visited Paapa in hospital. He could not talk but mustered up a smile when he saw me. Paapa finally succumbed to the call of the angels on February 24th, 2006. His funeral was touching. Afterwards, we went to the home of one of his daughters near Toronto and sang the many songs this great teacher, musician, and more. This man had lectured in Ghana, Nigeria, Uganda, U.S.A., Canada and I'm sure other places I don't know of.

His remains were eventually buried in Winneba, Ghana. During my first three years in Canada when I stayed with my brother, Paapa and I grew closer. He once said and I quote, "Marriage should be a five-year renewable contract." Wise words. This man is dearly missed.

Taking A Stranger To Africa

Anyone who is close to me knows I can't stand being called an African – especially when they know I'm from Ghana. I often point out to them that Africa has 1.3 billion people, spread over 54 countries and that there are over 3000 distinct languages. My argument is that by calling me an African, you have not taken the time to dig deeper and distinguish me from say a Kenyan or a South African. People will often break down Europe into countries but tend to paint all 1.3 billion Africans with one brush. Talk about stereotyping, right?

My return trips to Ghana and postings of photos had started drawing the attention of many people far and wide. That was no surprise. An acquaintance had expressed an interest in joining me on one of my trips so I set them up with my travel agent.

I learnt the hard way that sometimes going to Ghana/Africa for the first time with a stranger can be difficult. You don't know what their reaction to the place will be. You also don't know their previous travel experiences to compare what the long haul flights and cultures they are going to be exposed to will do to them. Because you don't know this person well, you are not in a position to let them know that their behaviour towards the "locals" is being perceived as rude, impolite or disturbing. The trip with this person had good and bad moments.

The 2008 trip with this stranger allowed me to spend a lot of time with my mother. She was in great spirits. We ate together. We talked a lot. I caught up with my Uncles and Aunts in Takoradi as well as Accra during this trip. I took a bus ride into the interior to Kumasi in the Ashanti Region. To Kwame Nkrumah University of Science and Technology...KNUST or "Tech" or short. This was the same university where my father had worked years back and where I had returned to obtain my degree in Architectural Design. I stayed at the lovely Engineering Guest House.

A cousin of mine who had been there for me when in my late teens I'd come up to the University before starting my under-grad studies, came to meet me. He was a Gulder beer man. I am a Star Lager man. We drank beer together. Going to "Tech" brought back great memories. I walked by Unity Hall where my residence was at the time. I took the trek from Unity Hall to the School of Architecture which I had done lots of times in my youth. I was not that young anymore and decided to take a cab back to the Engineering Guest House. It was great to reconnect with my past though.

Part of what made the trip exciting – besides escaping my "tour guide duties" - was just seeing the lush vegetation of Ghana on the five-hour bus ride to and from Accra. At that time some of the major highways were still under construction. Ghana was moving along.

When I returned from Kumasi, it was time to travel west with my guest. As most people from the diaspora do, my acquaintance visited Elmina Castle. The person was deeply moved by this as many people tend to be. I totally understood.

My relationship with the forts and castles in Ghana has always been distant. In my second year of secondary school, we had studied Ghanaian history. However, the teacher at the time was a young graduate who spent the period pontificating about his political views. He never talked about slavery. Slavery quite frankly had never been on my radar. It was out of boredom one day that I decided to visit Cape Coast Castle in my twenties. I was traumatized too and in the usual fashion, I wrote some poems.

Reflections at Cape Coast Castle

Adjoa Mansah

Adjoa Mansah!
Adjoa Mansah!
have you seen my son?
he went to fight for the village
the other men are back, but he is not

Adjoa Mansah!
Adjoa Mansah!
have you seen my son Kojo?
I fear he is a prisoner of war

A Little Light Please (from the slave quarters)

A little light, please
that's all I ask, O, Governor
for it's hot and stuffy in here
and all we have is this
one foot by one-foot aperture
and you choose to call it a window

A little light please, Sir Governor
for I can feel my neighbour's flesh
so close to mine
for you have crammed us like sardines
and we can barely breathe

A little light and space, O Governor
that's all I humbly ask
for I know in your quarters
you have far more light
you are far fewer in number
can you spare us poor slaves
a little more light, Sir Governor?

Any better?
Are we any better than them
those who came and enslaved
those who came and colonized
so many years now, they've been gone
yet our crimes are like theirs
for still we enslave one another
not in the name of nation, religion and race
but in the name of the tribe
still, we colonize one another
not from country to country
but the urban colonize the rural
the farmer sweats to feed us
and with the foreign exchange
the urban people amass wealth
and ignore the rural peasants

they came
they enslaved
they colonized
but are we better than them?
if not, why not?
let's take steps to become better
for they left us long ago

This journey back home to Ghana took me to Busua Beach in the Western Region to relax for a bit. This brought back fond memories of my childhood when a close Uncle would take all of us there. I've not been back to Busua Beach since. I re-visited the Kwame Nkrumah Mausoleum and Memorial Park in Accra which I had gone to before. On this second visit to the Mausoleum, Kwame Nkrumah's wife Fateyah been laid to rest next to him.

I made it back to Canada with my guest. After that experience, I've decided if I'm going to travel to Ghana or any other African country, I need to know them really well. My lesson has been learnt. Never take a stranger to Africa.

Here are photos from Elmina, my hometown.

The Voice On The Line

Oh, how the world has changed since the late 90's when I arrived in Canada! With family spread all over the world, we used to stay in touch mainly by phone. This meant huge long-distance bills. Then came the phone cards which helped bring down the cost of calls. Back in those days we used postcards, letters and had more human contact. Then came the advent of personal computers and the Internet. I got my first personal computer in 1996. It was an AST computer. If memory serves me right, the hard drive had 1.19 GB. I had gotten it at a Future Shop in Toronto. In my early days in Canada, I'd see the Future Shop sale signs every weekend. It took me a while to know that this was a regular thing and not a one-off. Before I bought my PC, I had an electronic typewriter. As I've been a writer since my mid 20's that device was one of the first things I bought in Canada.

Amazing how things have evolved since 1996. Families and friends around the world keep posted about each other's doings on social media. Let me rephrase that. We share what we want the world to see on social media. Some of us keep part of our lives private. Facebook which was at first for the young ones was taken over by those of us who are a little more 'seasoned'. WhatsApp has now taken over phone cards. That's how the world is now. Sometimes I do yearn for the good old days, but one wonders how good they really were. Hindsight is 20-20. Nostalgia has a way of making us re-write the past.

Staying in touch with my dearest mother has always done by

phone. Much as she has always known about computers, my mother has never been computer savvy. I've always relished hearing her strong voice. I find it reassuring. My mother's voice has always been clear and strong. Her mind always there. However, over the years it became clear that her mind and memory were fading. The conversations on the phone became harder to comprehend. After one of those difficult conversations, I had a discussion with my brother. I decided that it was time to go and spend time with my mother before illness robbed her of all her memories. I was ready to head back to Ghana again - where my mother who is my heart, lay beating.

Making Memories
With Mummy

I have too many memories of flying across the African continent to recount all of them in this book.

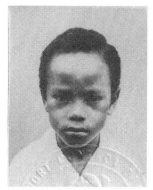

The above photo was from my first passport when I was about to turn six in the late '60s. My father, my older brother, older sister and I were leaving Ghana to start a new life in Zambia. Daddy left Ghana due to political reasons. He would later come back to Ghana to retire.

Some of the rituals around flying as children were around packing

and weighing out check-in luggage. We would fill our suitcases until they were almost bursting, then dance on them, then barely close them up. We would always arrive early at the airport for Dad to negotiate any overweight baggage payments that had to be made or not made. I'm not sure what Dad said to the folks at the check-in at the airports, but our suitcases always got on. As a child, I knew that there was no problem I faced that my father could not solve.

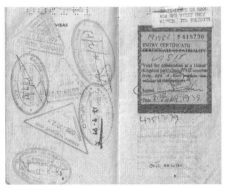

I remember many flights across the continent in planes that seemed to be stitched together by a thread. When the landing gear was being put in place before touchdown, you'd hear creeks and cranking and hope that everything was fine. We often flew across the continent on Ethiopian Airlines. Their planes had a fantastic safety record, but boy they sure were old back then. If there were delays in their flights coming from Asia, these would trickle down to us in West Africa. Those are my early memories of flying. Ethiopian Airlines with its memorable slogan "Thirteen months of summer".

Fast forward to when I was leaving Accra in the late 1980s to Nairobi en route to Toronto. I boarded a modern Ethiopian Airlines Boeing 767 Jet. Their planes had vastly improved in "newness".

My airline of choice for travel to and from Ghana is KLM. That's the airline I came with first and after trying Lufthansa, British Airways and Delta Airlines, I've decided that my reliable, friendly dependable "bus" to Ghana is KLM. I've never had any issues with

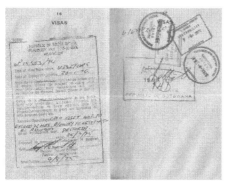

them. I used Lufthansa once. No problem there. Just that the air-fare was too high. When my father died in 1999 I went to and from Ghana with British Air-ways. I used them on my first trip to England when I was living in Kenya too around the age of seventeen. On recent trips to Ghana, it's become clear that they treat Ghanaians as though they were second class citizens. I'm not a fan of that. From what I've heard the same can be said of Brussels Air that relatively recently started flying to Ghana from Europe. I've never been able to afford to fly on Swiss Air. I hear they are an amazing airline. Recently Air France started going to Ghana and I'm a fan of theirs too. How about Delta Airlines?

Delta Airlines. On my first flight from Atlanta to Accra, we were delayed for five hours!!! Then they changed gate. I'm not sure if that meant the aircraft was changed. It was supposed to be a ten-hour flight on paper but it turned out to be eight. Thank God. Besides the delay and gate change, once we were air bourne, the Delta staff were not so generous with alcohol as the European Air-lines I was used to flying with had been. I had to go to the back of the plane to get more liquor when I craved a drop or two. Granted, that air travel has changed from back in the day when while flying in economy class, you were given loads of alcohol. But still flying cannot be that bad. I remember those days of air travel with fond-ness. I was once returning to Toronto from England on Canadian Airlines. An air hostess was walking down the aisle the plane with a bottle of red wine in one hand and a bottle of white wine in the other topping anybody up anyone who asked for more. That was my kind of air travel in the 1990s. On my second Delta flight to Ghana from JFK in New York City to Accra, I saw a bug between the panels of glass/plastic in the pothole. I wonder how it got there. My experience and stories I'd heard about Delta Airlines made me realize that that was it for me. I would not take this airline again unless I really had to. I read stories about their planes missing the runway by some distance. Then there are stories of untold delays. The funniest one was of someone carrying some stinky fish on the plane forcing them to land. Since all this happened, I've stuck to KLM and Air France. Each time I call my travel agent, he knows my preference. My travel agent - Royal Africa Travel at Islington and Albion is the best way to get to Ghana or Africa. That's their specialty and they do it well. I remember a friend who wanted to get to then war-torn Sierra Leone. Royal Africa Travel got them there and back to Toronto safely.

In April 2011, my dependable travel agents got me a good priced ticket with minimum transit time in Amsterdam as I headed to spend a month in Ghana to be with my beloved mother.

My one month in Ghana in April of 2011 is filled with many memories. Memories I made with my mother. Right after I arrived in Accra I spoke to Mummy on the phone. I did this for the whole month while I as in Ghana. I was either with her in person, or on the phone every single day of the trip. I was not able to go Takoradi right away because I had a commitment in Accra. I had made some literary inroads thanks to a connection I made on Facebook. I was the featured writer at the meeting of the Writer's Project at the Goethe Institute in Accra. I read from my chapbook called "Accra! Accra! More Poems About Modern Africans" which was well received. There was a lively discussion after the reading.

I headed to Takoradi soon after the reading to be with my mother. There was no driver or car on this trip. This time I took the large safe VIP buses across the coast. When I met Mummy, she was glad to see me. I told her about the reading and brought a copy of the chapbook for her. I read "Walking with Her" which she loved, then I gave her a copy of the chapbook. This was special as over the years I have written many poems for people but I rarely read these poems to them. My time with Mum was amazing that month. I wanted to take her out but she wasn't up for that.

Mummy would occasionally revert to her distant memories of her life from years ago. She knew who I was for the entire month and our conversations were deep. I was able to catch up with Aunts, Uncles and cousins too on this trip as I went back and forth along the coast between Accra and Takoradi. I decided on this trip that I wanted to start wearing a piece of jewelry that my mother had touched. On one of my jaunts to Accra, I had a silver ring custom made with the *gye nyame** symbol on it.

I brought it to my mother and had her place it on my right hand on the ring finger. I suggested to Mummy that we take a picture of us together with the ring. "I can't take the picture now until I have my wig set and I put it on."

Mother's mind had gone back to the prime of her life when she loved her wigs. We compromised and I took a photo of our hands together. Her now feeble hands holding my strong hands. The tables had turned. In my childhood, my hands were weak. She was always strong for me. Now it was my turn to hold her hand. I started wearing the ring from then onwards for many years.

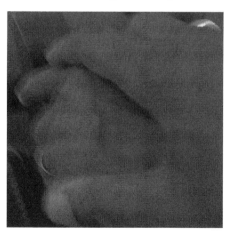

This was a month of catching up, bonding and feeling closer to the woman I call "my dear"...My dearest. There was a certain sense of urgency because we know that once a person starts losing their memory, we lose a part of them. One of the other meaningful memories of this trip that remains ingrained in me was my last meal with Mummy. Mummy loved her *fufu* with light soup. Her caregiver had made some for her that afternoon. I would soon be heading towards Accra. She ate her fufu from the bowl then asked me to put my hand in the bowl and eat with her. I felt closer to Mummy than I had ever. Mummy abruptly stopped eating. She was alert. Fully present. She blessed me. "You are my dearest son. You should be strong and you will do well in your life. God will continue to bless you always."

Soon after we had eaten and bonded, the taxi driver who would be taking me eastbound arrived. Saying my very last goodbye after a month in Ghana where I spent with Mummy was painful. I stood at the door of her home. Mummy clearly didn't want me to leave. I didn't want to go. Her caregiver said, "It's okay to leave. This happens all the time with your Mum. She never wants her guests to leave." I hugged my now smaller framed mother one last time as the taxi driver I was paying handsomely for the charter was getting impatient. Her body was frailer now. Her mind was coming and going. My strong woman, my protector and spiritual strength was not so strong. Her mortality was staring me in the face. The ride from Takoradi to Elmina where I wanted to spend one night before heading to Accra was tough. I am grateful to this day for that month of making Mummy Memories. I will always treasure them.

Gye Nyame means "except for God," symbolizes God's omnipotence through the knowledge that people should not fear anything except for God. ... Gye Nyame indicates the recognition of the supremacy of God over all beings and therefore is the one that is feared and revered by all.

**fufu is white and sticky (if plantain is not mixed with the cassava when pounding).*

Milestones In Canada

After over three decades of being an immigrant to Canada, there are many occasions and milestones that stand out. Join me in celebrating a few of these.

March 19th, 1989. One of my happiest moments was seeing my brother and his wife at Pearson International Airport after finishing arrival procedures. Here is a photo from the Ghanaian passport I arrived with.

This was my first and only car that I've owned. I bought it in the fall of 1990. The Canadian dream was unfolding.

Becoming a Canadian citizen remains one of the most special days of my stay in Canada, my new home. This happened just over three years after my arrival.

Commemoration of Canadian Citizenship

Commémoration de Citoyenneté Canadienne

When I turned forty I decided to live it up. I dressed up, rented a Limo and picked up four of my closest friends – two men and two women. We celebrated this milestone in style.

On June 18th, 2010, the lights went down and my first staged play started to a packed house. This was after six weeks of intense rehearsals.

Da Yie Me Mame

Sleep well my mother

T he most painful experience I have had since migrating to Canada is one that transcends my life here. It connected me with Ghana and the woman who birthed me. My dearest beloved one and only Mummy. The experience was tough but I'm most grateful for how things unfolded. When I heard that my mother wanted to see me as her time on earth was coming to a close, I was able to rush back to Ghana and be at my mother's bedside. I saw her frail body and touched her, whispered in her ear – in Fanti, my mother tongue - "Mummy, I'm here. I heard you wanted to see me. I have come. I have brought your favourite Yardley powder, Cocoa butter body cream, Classic scented cologne – Elizabeth Arden. Everything I know you want My Dear. I am here. I have come. " I held her fragile hand and prayed her into Psalm 91 in the Amplified Bible which starts with these words. *"He who dwells in the shelter of the Most High Will remain secure and rest in the shadow of the Almighty [whose power no enemy can withstand]. I will say of the Lord, "He is my refuge and my fortress, My God, in whom I trust [with great confidence, and on whom I rely]!*

Around her bed that evening at Takoradi along with me was her brother, his wife, Mummy's current caregiver and the new caregiver. The current caregiver who Mummy was fond of was about to leave on maternity leave. My mother had been in a diabetic coma for a few days. We spent that evening sharing our "Mummy stories". It was a light yet solemn time. I hoped against hope that Mummy would come out of the coma. I had come to Ghana prepared to visit my mother every day at the hospital until she was nursed back to health. I came armed with whatever funds it would take to give her the best care money could buy. When we were leaving the clinic, I left the Bible that I had brought and prayed from next to my Mother's pillow. I told one of the nurses, "Take care of my Mother. She's all I've got."

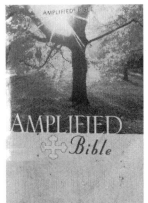

I was later told that the morning after, on a sunny Sunday 15th April 2012, the clinic staff bathed Mummy and groomed her with all her favourite things that I had brought for her. At 8.30 a.m., Mummy's voice on earth was silenced. She went to sing with the angels in the choirs of heaven. Going back to that place today brings tears to my eyes.

Shocking to think that just eight days before I had no intention of rushing back to Ghana. The circumstances leading up to my return started then. It was the Saturday before Easter 2012. My mother's health had been deteriorating – mainly due to diabetes. As a family, we were doing the best we could for my mother. My last full conversation I had had over the phone with my mother was in March, a few weeks before. I had just started working at a new location at my day job. I called her from a subway station. She seemed well. From that point on, Mummy's health had not gone too well. She had gotten weak and it was hard to monitor her insulin/sugar levels. Don't ask me for the details. I'm not a doctor. I had dinner with two close friends on that Saturday before Easter. We discussed the fact that sometimes when a person is ready to die, they wait to see someone before they leave earth. The next day was Easter Sunday. I cried like a baby all alone in my luxury condominium saying to God "I don't want my mother to die! I don't want my mother to die!" In that period of my life, I played the Boyz2Men "Song for Mama" over and over again. The lyrics reminded me of how close I was to my mother and how much she meant to me. That song saw me through that dark period. On the same Easter Sunday my two adopted Aunties who live across the street from our house in Accra called. They had gotten word that whenever my mother was told that I was coming to see her, she lit up. I knew then that Mummy wanted to see me. God had found a way to get this message to me. The next day on a Monday, I called my contact at Royal Africa Travel. I told them that I needed to go to Ghana by the end of the week. He said it was possible and introduced me to something called the express Visa from the Ghana High Commission Consular Office. I'd never heard of this until then. Before then it took about a week for me to get Ghana visas. I had initially told the travel agent that I wanted to leave on that Friday, however, I got word from Takoradi that Mummy's condition was not good. She appeared to be slipping into another diabetic coma. The precariousness of my mother's condition made me realize that I had to get to Ghana as soon as possible. Every day counted. I went into the office of the Supervisor at the new work location I had just started at. I told her what I was going through with tears streaming down my eyes. Without hesitation she said, "You have to go," and approved my vacation request. I called the travel agent who got me one of the two remaining seats in Economy Class on a KLM flight on that Thursday to Amsterdam – for my transit to Accra. I called Mummy's very pregnant caregiver on that Wednesday. Even though Mummy could not speak, she was alert and I was encouraged to talk to her.

"Mummy," I said with a tone of desperation. "Wait for me, I'm coming – with all the things I know you love". Mummy mustered the strength to cough. That was her way of saying "Yes."

Before my trip, many family members heard about the mission I was embarking on. They called to wish me the best. My dearest niece was amongst them. "Thanks for going on our behalf Uncle.

Tell Grandma I love her." My brother's wife also called. I bumped into a neighbour at my condo building from Asia. I told him about the trip I was about to take. He said in their culture getting the blessing of a person just before they passed away is an honour.

As you can imagine, the flight to Amsterdam was stressful. When I got to Amsterdam, I checked what was happening in Ghana via emails and social media. Mummy was still alive. The flight from Amsterdam to Accra was on Friday 13th of April 2012. For me that Friday was filled with nothing but God's blessings and good luck. When I got to Accra, my close friend and former roommate met with me. He is a medical doctor and thanks to his intervention, Mummy had been moved to a private hospital from a public one. He had gotten a local specialist doctor to visit my mother. We were all optimistic that Mummy would come out of the diabetic coma.

The four-hour bus ride to Takoradi took forever on Saturday, April 14th, 2012. I was warned that Mummy did not look that well. I did not care. I wasn't sure what I was going to do when I saw my mother. I just knew I had to get there. The new caregiver said she saw Mummy blink when I walked into her hospital room. There she lay on the bed. The strong woman who had been my strength looked fragile. I could see she was breathing. She was still alive. That's all that mattered to me. God and had heard my prayer. Mother had waited for me. My mother passed a few weeks before she turned 81. One of her favourite Psalms was 90. Verse ten of that Psalm reads "The days of our life are seventy years—Or even, if because of strength, eighty years". Mummy had claimed and lived that promise.

Eternity
May the angels of God
Carry you into Abraham's bosom
May the light of Jesus
Guide you on your journey
From this world to the one where there is life eternal

May the saints throw petals at your feet
As you walk through the pearly gates
To live forever with Jesus and all the other saints in Christ

They say, ye be ye bi, y'an be ye naira   (We came to
do some, not everything)
You not only did some, you did a hell of a lot
And you have left your mark on the souls
Of your birth children and the many
Who love to call you Mamma

Now rest my sweet mother
Rest well eternally
For your work on earth
Is done and now it starts
in the world beyond the grave
And will last for eternity

I spent two weeks in Ghana on that trip. I had seen my mother alive on Saturday. Touched her warm body when they brought her out of the clinic and onto the hearse the evening she died on Sunday. On Monday, I saw her mortal remains on a morgue table before was embalmed until her funeral. Ironically the hospital morgue where mother's body was stored was the same hospital where as a child, my mother would take me up and down the hallways trying to find cures for my many asthma-related skin rashes.

The day after Mummy passed away, the Senior Pastor from the Evangelical Church she attended came home. He explained how my mother had been a strong member of the church and that they would help with the funeral.

There were many family meetings and rituals around the death of my mother that I had to attend. My Uncle who had been close to my mother and was at her bedside was there to guide me through these meetings. I did not like most of these Fanti gatherings with strangers I did not know or particularly care about. One family ritual I enjoyed was called *"Nda Awotwe"* or eight days. This is when the family gathers a week after a person passes away to decide what has to be done. It was a small group of close and extended family members. My Uncle took the lead as usual. In the past, this was when families would make plans about how to bear the funeral costs. In this case, the refrain was simple. "The children would take care of everything." That was said over and over again.

Two months after my return to Canada, I went back to Ghana for my mother's funeral where all my siblings and extended family, friends, well-wishers and many others were present. We buried my mother under a tree in the cemetery outside Takoradi. The Pastor from her church led all the burial rituals and prayers. It started to rain right after Mummy's casket was lowered into the ground. The Sunday Thanksgiving Service at Mummy's Evangelical Christan church the day after her burial was heartwarming. We then came home for a social gathering where I got very drunk. I was allowed to. I had just buried my one and only dearest mother.

Today I Buried My Mother
Today we buried my mother under a tree
We, her children, siblings, family members, clan members and friends
Gathered to remember her, respect her, pay tribute to her

Today I saw the mortal remains of my mother sent back to the dust
That we all come from and all must go back to
It was a time to celebrate over eight decades of life on earth
And share memories of her, what she'd done and said
It was a time of sadness, laughter, singing, and bonding

Today we buried my mother under a tree
Outside the city where she grew up and lived and worked
And left the fragrance of her life
Yes, much as we have buried her mortal remains

Under a tree outside Takoradi
The fragrance of her well-lived life
Will forever be a part of our lives

On every single trip I have made to Ghana since then, I go and see my mother's grave. I make sure her grave is being maintained. I sprinkle her favourite powder over the grave. My mother will live in my heart forever.

A Poetic Interlude

nd now a poetic interlude featuring three of my favourites.

<u>African Dawns</u>

Sore! Sore! (Wake up! Wake up!)
Takoradi, Ghana 1973

Sore! Sore!
Wake up! Wake up!
Stirring up from a fitful sleep
on the kete, the grass prayer mat
waking up from dreams or nightmares
of witches and wizards and the supernatural
thankful that my soul wasn't taken from me in sleep
my mother nudges me as she wakes up
from her bed above
"Sore! Sore! Waa bo non nsiah"
"Wake up! Wake up! It's six o'clock"

"It's Cold Outside"   *Maseru, Lesotho*
July 1976

"Don't forget to make your bed
bed sheet over blanket, then bed sheet and
blanket and tuck in the sides and lay the
bedspread over everything
Oh! And remember to wear your sweater and gloves
It's really cold outside..."

Somewhere in Lesotho in the mid 1970's

Breakfast in Bed
Nairobi, Kenya 1979

Feeling kinda lazy tonight
don't wanna get out of bed
think I'll do what the 'bwana kubwa' does
I open my bedroom window
and yell out to the kitchen below
to Godwin, the faithful house boy
"Godwin, can you bring me breakfast today?"
"Yes bwana Kwame. what do you want?"
hmmm, I contemplate for a few moments
"Fried eggs, bacon and toast...with some tea please"
"Yes bwana Kwame, I'll have it up in about half an hour"
"Thanks, Godwin," as I say, close the window

and get back under the covers...to snooze a little more

The Path of the Righteous
Mombasa, Kenya 1984

the distant sunshine
over the Indian Ocean shines a light
yet I cannot see in front of me
far away though, I see the dawn breaking
"the path of the righteous
is like the light of dawn
that shines brighter and brighter
until the full day"
yes, in reflecting on dawn,
the scripture comes alive
yes, as the dawn breaks forth
the path in front of me
will become clear

Morning Release
Kyekyewere, Ghana 1987

scratching my eyes, stretching my hands
only to touch the body of my teammate
I wrap my sleeping cloth around me
slip-on my 'charlie wote' and head out
the smell of damp earth mixed with the taste of urine,
fresh morning dew on green grass and shrubs
I find the closest wall and release a gallon of piss
finding sweet relief in the morning release
I wrap my cloth around me and head back inside
finding yesterday's chewing stick,
and head for the stream
getting ready to start
another day of work with the team
and the people of Kyekyewere

Dance of Love

We are dancing our love
like two dancers on a stage
each one taking their step in turn
dancing to the rhythm of a tune
a tune not heard but felt
the tune of love in our hearts

So we dance, on and on
each in perfect motion
a true duet

Yet even as we dance
we ask ourselves
where will the dance take us?
will it go on forever and ever?
or will the music of love stop
and leave us apart?

Mangoes and Juice

when I feel the urge
to suck on something
something that's juicy
and tasty and has a tropical zest I reach for a mango

I love my mangoes
not too ripe, not too unripe
kinda yellow, kinda orange
not too hard, not too soft just kinda firm

I love to suck on my mango
drink in all the thick sticky juices
and even let some on fingers then lick it all off

every now and then
I wonder what kind of juice
you like to suck on
care to share with me?

what you like to do
when you feel like
having something
juicy, tasty, zesty,
and tropical?

for now, I guess
I'll stick to my mangoes
mangoes and juices
yellow, orange
kinda soft, kinda hard
just firm and nice to touch

The Business With Business Class

It happened to me on a whim. In 2009 I had started going to Montreal every summer for a weekend. I'd go to enjoy the French influence in a Canadian city that was English enough for me not to get totally lost. I loved the St. Hubert Chicken amongst other things. Over the years, I've done the Montreal City Bus Tour twice. This guided tour takes you to major sites including the Notre Dame Cathedral in the Old City of Montreal, the Olympic Stadium, Mount Royal Lookout and St. Joseph's Oratory. You are able to get off the bus at a few locations for a short period of time. I have taken some amazing photos over.

Initially, I'd go on these Montreal trips using a Megabus from Toronto. Then I started travel on VIA Rail trains. An acquaintance suggested that I go to Montreal by Business Class on the Via Rail train as a treat to myself. I loved the experience. The Departure Lounge. Boarding the train before the masses got on. The large comfortable seats in the train. The meal on board the train was like what you'd be served on an economy class plane flight. On my way back from one of the business class train trips, I called my Travel Agent. I asked him to look into how much it would cost for me to fly to Ghana by business class. If the upgrade on the train was this good, I could only imagine what business class by air would be like.

My travel agent eventually made this work within my budget. His suggestion was that I fly out to Ghana in Economy Class and come back by Business Class. In 2014 I had my first taste of flying Business Class on KLM from Accra. It was quite the experience. It started at the airport in Accra. After leaving passport control, I arrogantly joined the shorter "Business Class" line to have my baggage screened. I had been given more check-in baggage and carry on weight allowances. I then got to enjoy the exclusive Business Class lounge. Every airport has some of these. I didn't know about them until my eyes were opened and I became a "member". The three-hour wait for departure in the airport was not on one of those famously uncomfortable airport chairs. I think someone designs those chairs to make them uncomfortable so you don't sleep and miss your flight. I had a buffet of food and unlimited alcohol to drink as I waited to board. I didn't have to pay for a drink at some bar in the airport terminal – and maybe sit next to a lonely stranger who wanted someone to chat with. In the Business Class lounge, everyone seemed "uppity" and "sophisticated". This high life was worth a taste and I recommend it to everyone. I later got to experience Business Class Lounges in Toronto and Amsterdam.

In Toronto, Business Class passengers board before economy passengers. That's why you see these seemingly important people sitting in their huge cot-like chairs as we peasants head to economy class at the back of the plane. In Ghana, they let the Economy Class passengers board before we "the elders" come and take our seats in Business Class. Once you are on board and sit on the wide seat that flattens into a bed, you are handed a headset that reminds me of the Bose Quiet Comfort ones. These have to be returned or left on your seat as you depart. You aren't given one of the flimsy earbuds they supply you economy and asked you to keep or throw away after use. The TV in front of me in my Business Class seat was huge! The concept of legroom was none existent...I had a small room like space all for myself.

 After relaxing in my seat, I was offered champaign or beer before taking off. The real treat started once we had reached cruising altitude...The stewards/stewardesses didn't come by with trays offering you chicken or fish. In Business Class I was given a high-end restaurant menu and asked what my preference was. It was like they had a chef in the air. Maybe they did. I don't know. I was served with fine China and stainless steel cutlery...I feasted on a five-course dinner. The food kept coming and coming and coming. Like any good waitress, the stewardess assigned to me had noted my preferred alcoholic beverage and kept bringing me more. After dinner, she came in to check if I enjoyed my meal. She'd occasionally check on me all flight long calling me by my name.

When I was about to leave the plane, I was asked to select a ceramic house as a token of appreciation. So, that's what my Uncle in Takoradi was displaying in his living room! Evidence that he's flow business class with KLM before. I have never asked him. He is a well-travelled man.

this side of heaven

this side of heaven
let me know what it feels like
to live in the lap of luxury
to taste what others who live
in true wealth experience

this side of heaven
before I go and join the angels
and our long lost ancestors who have gone before us
let me feel the warmth and tender kisses of another human
who wants me as much as I want them
and who wants us to hold on and never let each other go

this side of heaven
before I go and join the realms of the spiritual world
I want to travel and see lots places on the earth
I want to be able to fly as though I owned the airline
then walk in the dirt and poverty of a slum
I want to dine with princes and walk with paupers
I want to bond with people who think they are smart
and those who don't know how smart they are

this side of heaven
right here on earth while I have breath and life and health
I want to suck the marrow of life dry and enjoy every second of
my journey
so when my time comes...and it will come...for none of us will live
this side of heaven forever

I want my journey to be rich and worthwhile, full of many journeys
so that when I go to the other side of heaven
I'll report to them that my stay this side of heaven
was truly worth it.

After that one taste of Business Class, it was hard to go back to flying economy. However, the reality of my wallet had made this necessary. How does a man get a taste of heaven on earth then come back to earth? I had no choice. Looking at the small ceramic houses in my living  room and factoring in the one I gave away, I've flown five business class trips. That means since my first two-flight experience I've enjoyed the luxury of this experience three times. I've done the odd one leg flight by paying for an upgrade at the last minute or when it was possible, bidding for business class seats. It's been a few years since I enjoyed "a taste of heaven". I hope to get it again soon.

My basic requirements for flying have changed. In the sixties when I started travelling a seat was just a seat on a plane. You had a window, middle or aisle seat. Nowadays, to get more comfortable seats you have to upgrade your base ticket price. After over three decades of working in Canada, I have decided that I will only travel at a minimum in Economy Comfort seats. This is situated just behind the Business Class Cabin. Of course, you get more legroom. In addition to being Economy Comfort seating, whenever I can, I will order and "a la carte" meal. Having these meals has allowed me to have a business class meal while languishing in economy. At one time you could order these "better than economy class meals" from a relatively small fee. The eligible flights that you can order these meals on have decreased over the years. Recently I ordered the "Champagne Delight Meal."

About a year ago, I was waiting in line to check-in at Pearson International Airport when an air hostess began selling tickets to use the Business class lounge for about thirty dollars. I said yes and that too is something I have decided to treat myself to each time I fly. If I can pay a bit of money to use the Business Class Lounge in all airports, then why not? So that's the scoop on the business about Business Class. Happy safe flights to everyone.

Akwaaba...Welcome

To Ghana...A front row view

We are on board a KLM flight that took from Amsterdam. The pilot has just announced that we are on the approach to Kotoka International Airport, Accra. In an hour we will be landing. I've been on this plane for about six hours. I left Toronto some seventeen hours ago. I've gone through about five time zones east of Toronto. Luckily, I'm one of those people who can sleep on flights so I've had some rest. Being in Economy Comfort has given me more legroom but I still long for the next time I can afford to be in Business Class.

Planning a trip to Ghana is always a big thing for me. Everything has led up to this moment. Picking my travel dates. Getting the time off from work. Contacting Royal Africa Travel to see what my options are. They know that I don't like being in transit for more than three hours. One time on a trip from Ghana I was stuck at the airport in Frankfurt for thirteen hours. That was torcher.

As the plane gradually reduces altitude, my excitement wells up taking over the fatigue of travel. I'll soon be at home. Well, one of my homes. This is the country where I have roots going back way beyond my life. This is where I have Aunts, Uncles and my parents both resting eternally. Sometimes starting over seventeen hours of travel can be daunting. With landing at Accra getting closer and closer, I feel the excitement, joy, anticipation of what lies ahead.

What makes this trip special too is that after over fifty years of travelling to and from Ghana, they have finally opened the new Terminal three. I will no longer have to walk down the stairs from the plane and embraced by a blanket of hot air and then be bussed to the airport terminal.

The plane has touched down. For some odd reason when the plane touches down in Ghana, sometimes people clap. As if the pilots did something amazing. They were just doing their job. However, with a plane full of mainly Ghanaians who boarded in Amsterdam, it's understood. Most of us are religious. We have finished taxing and are now able to walk through a tunnel into the terminal. I like what I see already. My trip through Immigration is fast. I'm a Canadian and Registered Dual Citizen. This is when I start blending in. I crack a joke with the Immigration officer in Fanti. Normally I say that despite the Canadian passport, I'm still Ghanaian. We laugh. There are some people of paler complexions around but they are the foreigners. They are the ones we should be asking "where you from originally?" For me, I can point to where my father's house is. This is home. No questions asked.

I'm being more impressed with this new terminal by the minute. It looks like any terminal in the Western world. While I'm waiting for my baggage – which comes relatively quickly - I turn on my Ghana phone. I've always had a Ghana phone. You need one in Ghana. Everyone calls or texts. Even illiterate guys have phones. I remember once a mechanic asking me to enter my number into his phone. It was clear he didn't know how to read or write. Clearly, he knew numbers. I call my two "Aunties" who live across the street where I will stay to let them know I've arrived safely. Every time I go to Ghana, they welcome me with a home-cooked meal. It's good to hear their voices.

Once I'm about to leave the airport terminal, I ask where the Co-op Taxis are now stationed that there's a new terminal. There was a time when I was met at the airport by a friend or someone. With my more frequent visits since 2012, I make it a point to bring back enough Ghanaian Cedis (currency) to cover my taxi trip home. I don't trust every taxi driver in Ghana. Over the years, I have used the same taxi rank. The Co-op Taxis. They have set rates to different destinations and will get me home safely. They are a little pricier than other taxis though. A man takes my baggage on the bus to the old terminal where the taxi rank is. Eventually, we are on our way home. Even though it's dark, I know the route from the airport to my destination. The radio is on in the taxi. The station is playing hip-life music. The radio host is speaking in Twi. Truly this is home. There's lots of English all around. However, there's also a ton of stuff in Ghanaian languages everywhere. The taxi driver is engaging me in small talk. How my trip was. Where I came from. How long I'll be here. I indulge him and answer all his questions. I like that about Ghana. For the next three weeks that I am here, I will never feel lonely. There will be way more social interaction amongst friends and strangers that I will have in ten years in North America.

We are soon at home. The driver unloads the stuff and leaves it outside the gate. I pay him, giving him an extra tip. After settling into the house with the help of the caregiver, I shower and freshen up. I go across the street to my two Aunties who are waiting for me. They have been chilling a Star Lager all day long. They know that's what I like. I wait with curiosity at what they have cooked for me. As they lay out the spread on the verandah where the breeze is good, I give them the gifts I brought. Trinkets to say "I thought about you" from Canada. There was a time in my childhood when we would travel and bring gifts because all the stores were bare. Not nowadays. Ghana has everything but I still believe in giving small gifts as gestures.

The food is now ready. My Aunties made some boiled yams with palava sauce (cocoyam leaves). There's everything in the stew...meat, fish, chicken and more...soaked palm oil. I normally gain 10 pounds on this three-week trip. As I eat and we talk and we reflect. Time has already started to slow down. I've left the fast-paced time-sensitive North Amerian life I am decompressing. Feels so good to be home.

The next three weeks are going to be full as I reach out to my sister, uncles, aunts, friends, family and many others. I will go on a food tour. I'll eat all the Ghanaian food that I can buy in the West End of Toronto but that I miss so badly. When I get bored with Ghanaian food, I'll find whatever Western food I want. For now though, I'm going on a binge. I'll visit my favourite restaurants and spots in Accra, Elmina, Cape Coast and Takoradi. I may even do a trip to Kumasi.

I'll enjoy live music at +233 Bar and Grill. I'll have their amazing kebabs -lamb or chicken. I will go to The Republic at Osu for karaoke night or any other night – where the street is blocked and you literally sit on the road.

On this trip, I will discover a new favourite venue called Afrikko

at Danquah Circle. In Elmina, I'll have a grilled tilapia as I listen to the waves of the Atlantic Ocean close by at Mabel's table. I will not watch a lot of television. Just listen to the radio most of the time. When in Accra my station of choice is Citi Fm 97.3. When I'm in Takoradi, after I have greeted my living Uncles and Aunts, I will visit my mother's grave to make sure it's being kept well.

I'll go up to Harbourview for a Star Beer. Whether I spend the night in Takoradi, head back to Elmina or Accra all depends on several things. On when I got to Takoradi, how I feel and so much

more. I'm on vacation now. Nothing is set in stone. I'm here to relax, unwind and enjoy the sweetness of being in Ghana. I'll make cherished memories that I'll keep with me to see me through the next long winter in Canada.

Dual Citizen

With each of my ever-increasing trips to Ghana on a Canadian passport, I had to get a visa each time. My travel agent had planted the idea of me becoming a Registered Dual Citizen in Ghana earlier but I had ignored him. On my trip to Ghana in October 2016, I Googled the process to obtain this status online and decided to go to the Ministry of Interior early one week. I was there before 8.00 a.m. I was signed in and waited my turn to be served.

I was pleasantly surprised at the level of efficiency I was provided with. The civil servant I met told me what forms needed to be filled, what documents I needed and fees required. Over three weeks, I was able to get everything in order. When I went back to the Ministry of Interior Office weeks later, I had made some errors in obtaining certain documents. The same person I'd met earlier told me what steps to take to correct this. Despite the impressions I had had about inefficiency, bribery and corruption in Ghana, I did not experience these in my dealings with this Ministry. Everything went well. I could have been in a Canadian government office for all I cared. Since becoming a registered Dual Citizen in Ghana, I do not require a visa to enter Ghana each time. That is a relief. One less thing to deal with.

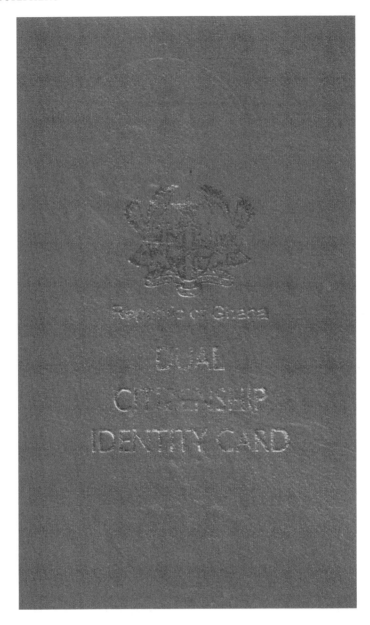

Post Script

I started this memoir as a man in his late twenties coming to a land that was going to be home. I was tired of travelling from place to place. Canada was going to be the place where I planted my roots. With time though, my connection to Ghana has strengthened. It's like the longer I stayed here and grew older, the more I wanted to connect with where everything started. I have strong connections to Canada but they are more recent in my life. I have deeper connections in Ghana going back way before I came into this world. Maybe this yearning for my roots is part of the reality of how I have changed. How the world has changed. I'm living in two countries at the same time. Finding myself at home in both places. One may say, I am more than a dual citizen. I started as a Ghanaian. Became Canadian. I am a Dual Citizen but I'm also one of many world citizens. What a journey that continues.

Kwame Stephens

 **K**wame Stephens is an author, playwright and poet who migrated to Canada over three decades ago. Prior to this Kwame lived in Ghana, Kenya and Zambia. He also travelled in seven other African countries. Kwame now finds himself torn between living in Ghana and Canada. Kwame's books are available on Amazon.com and related websites. These include *The Prophet's Room and Other Modern African Stories*, *Nymipa - A Collection of Poems* and *Dark Hard Chocolate Stories*. Beyond being an author, Kwame is a public speaker, performer, facilitator and educator. Kwame occasionally blogs at kwamestephens.blogspot.com. He can be reached by email at kwame_stephens@rogers.com.

Printed in Great Britain
by Amazon

10128633R00050